SNAPSHOTS

FROM A

LOVE AFFAIR

SELECTED POEMS

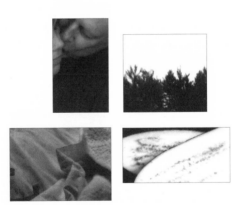

for each woman who has loved me

and for all the others, too

SNAPSHOTS FROM A LOVE AFFAIR

SELECTED POEMS

NORMAN ABELSON

PHOTOGRAPHS

WENDY CAHILL

ACKNOWLEDGEMENTS

Writing this book was a pleasure, a round-up of memory, consolidation of reverie, fantasy, romantic flights and painful crashes. But, I discovered there was still much to be done after the writing was complete.

I had so much help getting from there to here, and I want to recognize the many contributions made to this volume by loved ones, friends and associates. My thanks and gratitude to:

Maggie van Galen, for many hours of toil, reading, suggesting, editing; Skye Alexander for perceptive editing and instruction; Mary Lou Nye for her sensitive and artistic design; members of my writing group – especially Erica Bodwell and Kellie Wardman O'Reilly – for their insight and daring honesty; Dina Abelson for the love and patience to allow me to experiment and grow; Wendy Cahill, my collaborator, for her kindness and her talent in bringing life and feeling to her pictures; and, finally, to the dear people in my life who have read my writing, a piece at a time, encouraging and sustaining me: Kari Lynge, Margaret Morrill, Bunny Shuman.

And my gratitude to the Spirit who planted the seeds that grew inside my heart and mind.

NORMAN ABELSON
Concord, New Hampshire
July 2000

C O N T E N T S

LYRICS FOR A LOVE AFFAIR

CONCLUSIONS

FOREWORD

REVEALED

I used to think
I'd go on forever,
feeding my poetry
to my fattening soul.

It was ace in the hole,
tucked away for a rainy day:
a hedge
against future's death.

Till I looked
in the split mirror
of infinity
and found I dying,
day by day.

Therefore, this.

SNAPSHOTS FROM A LOVE AFFAIR

BEGINNINGS

Was she there that August day in 1943?
He tried so hard to remember, reconstruct.

He thought he could see her
folded small behind her daddy;

he thought he could see her,
legs (in white socks) crossed,
peeping out shyly from the triangle
of dad's arm on hip.

He thought he saw her smile, head dropping,
turn and run to a woman standing,

dress blown by the wind,
across a brown grass field.

EPIPHANY

A not-very-good Greek salad
sat barely eaten; he soaked
a paper napkin in water to
loose the oily drops of dressing
spilled in his lap.

She wasn't eating,
moving around the cafeteria's perimeter
arms folded across her back
looking at prints along the walls.

It was mid-afternoon.
The place was empty.
He fell in love.

SALE

You loved it!
Five for the price of four.

"I'm such a cheapskate," you
say proudly, showering me with
your unheard of generosity;
you embarrassed by the act of giving.

Finally, nothing more to give,
you give me you.

3/2

From the driver's seat she dropped
her head in his lap.
"Kiss me," she whispered,
his mouth already moving to hers.

So many meetings, proper, friendly,
frightening, unfulfilled;
changed forever in that moment
as a pickup parked beside.

Blind and deaf to trees and trucks,
their music was the riff of a zipper;
his hand found her breast,
sealed them together.

PASSION

They moved hurriedly
up the narrow staircase,
passion rising,
freeing buttons & zippers
touching   &   feeling on the way.

Suddenly   unreasonably
they stopped
sat
talked for an hour
about music/art/love.

A PERFECT FIT

She slept quiet, unmoving.
They were close, but not touching.
Well, his fingertips were in that spot
where shoulder meets neck.

It was their first all-night together,
and she was nervous. ("Scared to death,"
she told him months later.)

He never told her how he felt:
Strange, new and, yes, scared.

On that night he came to understand
afterglow together was the loving
part of passion, when ardor moved
to tenderness, hardness and urgency
to softness.

He awoke in the morning to find her
smiling, nestled small in his arms.

AT A GLANCE

He can see from the end of the hall,
her:
in the shower, glass door ajar,
cheeks still flushed from lovemaking.

Steamy water cascades
down her shoulders and breasts,
one stream escaping,
puddled on the tiled floor.

A SURPRISE

The first time
they shared a
bathroom

was a beautiful
and unifying
experience.

FIRST LIGHT

Hurry, he whispers, the others still asleep.
She struggles, pulls the sweatshirt over
sleepy eyes. They glide, no sound,
through the sliding doors, invisible,
into thinning darkness.

Car moves alone, slowly, a turtle,
across the marsh. He prays to Ra:
"Hold back your entrance
so my love will see it all."

They take the sharp turn
to the ocean view
just as first rays stab
through hazy half-light.

It's so beautiful, dear," says
she, tears dropping. "Thank you."
He smiles, believing he had some
part in this diurnal display.

THEATER REVERIE

Mamet's locutions, strange
but brilliant, in the time of
powdered perukes, Empire waistlines.

In the plot:
echoes of Sappho,
buxom maids, lost jewelry,
mixed together as a hasty pudding.

Different drama in the orchestra seats:
lovers parted by aisle and row,
aliens apart.

The lovers demand:
"Change the script, David.
Put us together."

The actors are frozen on stage.

Mamet re-writes:
"Suddenly two empty seats

are spotted on the side, adjoining.
Lovers move to them; hold hands."

The play resumes.

GREEN LITE!

I saw you across the room
at the meeting
laughing as your hand
came to rest
on the sleeve of Jack's white shirt.

He looked up, smiling.
I hoped you would
find something not to
your liking. You told me
much later he had the wrong hands.
Not like mine.

Didn't worry as much about Frank,
not even when you lowered
your cheek for a kiss.
Not for you, that nice
disheveled man.

With the two sitting
close at your table,
you had histories.

You'd moved far past them,
I assured myself.
Being in love
ain't for sissies!

15

INTERTWININGS

a plastic cup
    filled to overflowing with the
    finest shiitake soup on earth
        shared with white plastic spoons
        at one of three tiny tables
    in that joint across from the park.

utter ecstasy.

and that doesn't even
count the french bread.

12:08 A.M.

He'd never questioned time or space
'til that ungodly first separation.

He'd known time had many cadences &
space was figured by differing measures.

        Now hours stretched to eons.
            space to light years.

        Minutes, even seconds,
        he explored for good news.

None.

ALPHA

Your head was low
    eyes closed
as you slid off the
    last of your clothing.

My secret longings
    before me
Waiting
    at my bidding.

I
    took in my breath
   to lung bottom.

Reached out
    took your hand.

DISCONNECTED

The phone
answer the phone.
Where are you?
Answer the phone.

Unconnected,
no one to help;
not AT&T information.
Why aren't you home?

O.K., I'll wait three minutes
then try again.
Three minutes,
I promise.

If you answer we'll
talk five minutes.
No more. I promise.
Answer the phone, darling.

I'll read your last letter again,
think about our last meeting,
look at the great picture of us,
take out the rubbish.

I'm going to call your office.
Can't do that. What if someone
else answers. Can't do that.

I'll just wait until you call me.
I know you will. Know it.
I'll wait an hour, get busy with
my own work. Then you'll call.

I hope you're all right, feeling
good. Maybe you're sick. Better
check. I'll try just once more.

PICTURES, AND MORE, AT AN EXHIBITION

They moved in opposite directions
around the gallery,

meeting before a huge canvas
they viewed with ambivalence.

✶ He: I like him more than I used to.
    She: He takes getting used to.

The plan was to meet by accident
two old acquaintances
art lovers
exchange views
part.

Then meet at her car.
After all, they had still
another hour and a half

together.

INTRUSION

One day she was ill.
She tried so hard to
fight it, hide it.

When sickness overcame her
she was ashamed, embarrassed.

> "This is the worst
> you'll ever see me.
> I'm strong. Don't
> ever think I'm not."

He was confused.
Should he leave,
comfort her,
what?

He sat in a chair away from her bed,
his pain quite different than hers.

BUMPS

They met, walked
past the pines to their pond.
Summer was long gone, and
so were the geese.

Dark water had frozen lightly
around the shore plants.
The frigid air was next to
painful to take in.

"It's just another bump on the road," he said.
"But it hurts too much when we're apart," she said.
"It's the only hand we've been dealt."
"You're right. Before you go, touch my face
the way you do."

REVELATION

She: Having everything but love
     is nothing.

He: Having love and nothing else
     is everything.

HAPPY ACCIDENT

"Ow, damn it, ow!"
He bumped into that same table edge in the dark.
Third time.

He was still learning her apartment.
There were no night lights.
He tried to illuminate the place in his mind,
but he forgot the table.

Now she was awake. "You O.K. love?"
"Sorry to wake you.
Bumped into that damn table again,
got me right in the groin."

"Come here. Let me kiss it for you."
Gifts, he decided, sometimes come in the strangest
wrapping.

IT'S NOT ALWAYS ABOUT ART & LITERATURE

Hon.
Yah?
Do you like eggplant?
Depends.
On what?
I love it in moussaka.
How about just plain?
Nope.
Will you try it plain?
Sure.
I love you.

ONLY

She was leaving   again.

Her phone voice was residually happy
from yesterday's hours together.

"It's only for a few days, hon," she said.
He knew. But each day broken into
counted hours and minutes
had no "only."

She knew that, of course,
but it was her turn
to be brave.

NINE-ONE-ONE

You're gone
and I'm . . . I'm what?
Lost, aimless
empty, unidentified

These several days
I'm where?
Ah, yeah: in suspended animation

Inanimate, not that I'm not
doing stuff and things;
even breathing occasionally

Lifeless, not that I'm not
alive; devoid of you

Off my life-support system.
I need you back to thwack me
with those high-charged paddles

One hand on my chest
the other over my heart, jolting,
yelling "I've got a pulse!"

WORTH THE WAIT

He watched her walking away from him.
She had told him to wait,
"I'll just be a minute in the store."

As her figure retreated, he shut one
eye for a telescope view. She seemed
to be closer.

She walked straight, like a lady,
no cheap rear-end wiggle. She turned,
smiled, waved, disappeared.

She came back, said she'd bought the sexy teddy
he had asked for, adding shyly:
"You can't see it until it's on."

IT TAKES TIME

Even after just two days apart, she is shy.
He: I love you.
She: Thank you, darling.

He says: You are so beautiful.
Her face drops, like a little girl told by an
aunt that she is cute.

He: I missed you.
She: Thank you, darling.

Twenty minutes pass. She is nestled
next to him, her face buried against
his shoulder. Comfortable now.

She whispers: I love you; I missed
you horribly.
He: Thank you, darling.

ANNIVERSARY

One of those corny candles
shaped like the number "1"
burning in a small ash tray;

They give each other cards
amazingly alike: how lucky they
are to have found each other,
and so on;

Small gifts exchanged,
small enough to be tucked
in pocket and purse;

Squeezing hugs, as much
in desperation as affection,
sweet kisses tinged with the blues;

a rumpled hotel bed in daylight
tells it all.

REALITY CHECK

"You see the moon last night?
It was spectacular."

"I can't see the moon when
we're not together."

"Really? Why?"

"I just don't look."

TWO THUMBS UP

They went to the movies
on a sunny afternoon.

It was Tuesday so
only a couple dozen people
were watching the
hugely popular film.

They both hated it.

Instead, they gave
an Oscar nomination to

Holding Hands In The Dark.

COFFEE AND . . .

That coffee shop was where
they talked about politics
and how their work had gone
since last time.

The leftover half rollup sandwich
he took home. The leftover
conversation she saved.

Always too much food.
Never enough time.

STILL STRANGERS

He saw her one day
          just for a moment
          at a time they weren't to meet
doing workday errands.

She opened her car door
got out hefting a large tote bag
wrestled a quarter out of her
stuffed purse, fed the meter

turned and went into a sports store.

He would have followed,
but wasn't sure he had the right.

FOUR DAYS: FOREVER?

"Can four days and nights together
be a forever?"

She doesn't ask easy questions;
he never answers quickly.

Webster informs him on forever: For eternity;
         for always;
         endlessly.

He informs her: "Yes, it can be a forever."

She says: "I knew it."

MORNING AFTER

An insistent knock on the door
of the small hotel, their private home.

"Come back to clean later," he yelled
from the bathroom.

Bang! Bang!

He remembered the chambermaids
spoke only Spanish. He went to the door
opened it inches
hiding his naked body.

It was she: Smiling, smug, about
her surprise. (She'd called only a
half hour before, on the way to work, she said.)

"How are you darling? Sleep O.K.?" in her
smallest voice.

He reached out, pulled her
in by the collar of her jacket.

"I missed you," she said, sobbing,
spilling tears
on his bare chest.

LYRICS FOR
A LOVE AFFAIR

MOVING TO AMARNA

Nefertiti what was your magic,
how did it feel to be you?

Did you guess these millennia later
we'd be gawking at your likenesses
in wonder and wondering?

I move close to my love
who resembles you, ask
if she feels your magic in her.

"Come," she answers, "make love to me.
It is woman's only way to teach
about Nefertiti."

"Words are a man's way. Come be
with me."

I lay the night against her regal
breast. And understood.

LUMIÉRE

Beauty flows from the space between
your cheekbone and the bottom eyelid.
Under the skin a sheen illumines
your face. Barely seen but there.
Near you, I reach out
to catch that elusive light.
Not able to capture the ethereal,
instead I touch you
You sigh softly giving in to my
finger-tips with a faint smile.

IN HER DIARY

I was there then, invisible.
All those times together.
Invisible.

You wrote secretly of love,
lust, life. Not a word of me
on any page.

With you at the dance
that junior prom. But
no dance shared, hands touching,
learning each other.

You popular, blossoming, being young.

Me locked inside a heart and mind
yearning but blocked.

Invisible.

SCARED

Will I believe you
when you say you need help?
Will I trust your crying out,
your fear, your angst?
Will you believe my untutored
stumblings, sweaty hands, my trying?
Will you do what I tell you,
even if you think I am wrong?
Will our friendship dim our love,
now, ever? Will it?

JOURNEY

As I know you deeper, I see
you through new eyes.

Spectral,
you move to & into my self,

there take root, our cells merging
two souls = one essence.

> Together, apart,
> never again
> separate or separated.

LIGHT AT DUSK

The moment is so brief and evanescent
yet when lit by the sparking embers of passion
becomes its own eternity.

You, then the searing heat of the sun, now
the cool healing moon goddess, Selene.

The light at dusk, violet gray,
a splattered palette of fading color.

In thickening darkness we mold a nest
for two hearts — weary, on guard against
an ice blue world — to warm, open like
nestlings' tiny beaks.

Moonlit, safe, with passion, tenderness, tears,
we proclaim, against all odds,
undying, unyielding love.

THIS OR THAT?

Would I give up two days with you
in the future
To have you come back to me
just one day sooner?

Today, with you so distant, I would
say, unreservedly, yes.
But then the one day would be gone
and the sacrifice of two days
apart would loom.

The plight of lovers
who belong every minute together
but cannot be.

ARE YOU LISTENING?

The philosopher admits:
Birth is an accident
Life is a crap-shoot
Death is unavoidable.

But love, that
is another story:
the transcendent Emerson
said if you do the thing
you will have the power.

We have the power to make
love beautiful and lasting
and life-affirming.

Love shows up one day on
the door-step of our libido
inches itself into our soul
and says Here I am; make what
you will of me.

But don't forsake or take me lightly.
I may not come your
way again — ever.

AT LAST ANOTHER

I grieved and you were there.
I needed, you provided.

I was alone and you came near.
I spoke sadness; you heard.

I was chilled, and you provided warmth.
My melancholy thoughts you read and erased.

At a time of ending you were a beginning.
Through the fog of death you were a beacon of life.

Your presence is my peace.

SERENADE

the world is so full
yet empty without you.
the ocean at sunrise
misses your eyes.

make your way to me.

my mind flows over
with idylls for you.
i dream of resting quiet
upon your breast.

make your way to me.

the flow of your shape
in my mind speeds my pulse
yet my arms are empty,
fingertips aching for your skin.

you are my joie de vivre;
make your way to me.

HAIKU OF LOVE

When the world does end
and time twists on forever
I want you with me.

Love, I will grow wings
to fly us to a new star.
Sit upon my back.

I have the power.
Risk your life, my love, with me;
we'll live forever.

Forever as one
we'll circle the universe
Together always.

LANAI

Talk to me of giant moon
of star-kissed eves and rippling tides
Tell me all of sunbathed beach
of coral shells and morning love.

Show me through your almond eyes
the pale white sand, the azure skies
Make me know all I have missed
an   orchid field, a midnight tryst
          on a darkened mountainside.

Let me feel that questing pulse
of many bloods within me mixed
Transport me across time and space
to your secret, far-off place.

Where I can loose this worried heart
unleash my caged-up dreams, and start
to live as man was meant to be
with an island girl beside the sea.

WE

I'm alone with all the rest,
yet I'm with everyone
when there's just us.

Together,
we are all of each other,
and no part of anyone else.

NIGHT VISION

The nape of your neck
crowns my midnight world;
framed by blanket top
and wild blonde hair,

glowing, shining
in my eyes,
even in the dark.

My passion rises with this light.
But I need not wake you,
I am sated merely by the sight.

WEDDING

there is no end of time for dreaming dreams
or sitting side by side next to the sea;
there is no chiming clock, whatever seems,
to knell the close of days 'tween thee and me.

i know no chariot race to earth's far end
nor any eagle soaring o'er high peak,
to move a rising heart by half again
as when our borning love began to speak.

we reached this day by no quick shortened route;
instead, we stand here, tried, as friend to friend.
we've smelled the blossoms, now we reap the fruit;
we've scaled the mountain, now the vale we'll
wend.

no, there is no end of time for dreaming dreams
or sitting side by side next to the sea;
to catch the fading sun, while yet it gleams,
assuring us of our eternity.

CARETAKERS

A tiny crack,
thin as a hair,
showed up,
as it might on
a fragile
Dresden tea-cup.

they were afraid,
each of them, to
call it to attention
lest its mere mention
might rend their love,
break them again into
the two halves they were.

see the crack, he asked
one day, tentatively.
it's very thin,   she
said, sighing.

it spoken, they knew their
love-cup was safe. they
would handle it more
gently from now on.

LOVE, ME

Is shabbat complete
without a piece of challah,
or Yom Kippur with it?

Is the menorah candle lit
before a drop of hot wax
wakens my fingers?

Am I real to you
when we're apart?

If not, what am I
this separated moment?

CONCLUSIONS

. . . AS SURELY AS DAY
FOLLOWS NIGHT . . .

I throw   my heart upon   the outing tide
knowing that in the classic, immutable
shape of things, it will return, as surely
as swell follows ebb; ebb, swell.

I lie softly on ten billion grains of sand,
they cushioned by ten billion billion more.
The sun which burned me half deep red is gone.

And now cool light glows on me,
naked on my endless sand bed,
but the tide revolts against
its timeless mistress, Moon,
ignoring her magnetic demand.

It goes and goes, never to return,
serving up my heart to someone, somewhere.
I rise in pain, having given away
that which I believed I only had lent.

FARE THEE WELL

For a fleeting time
we sped together
through a dream,
fearing soon the morning sun
would heat our eyes awake.

No voice did we allow
to pierce our slumbered love,
and, smiling, walked that
star-splashed world as if alone.

But morn must have its way with us
do what we would,
and, lacking pity, pushed aside
our veil of dark.

Then as the warming rays
lit up our waning eve,
we woke with stretching sighs
to find our dream was done.

IT CAN'T BE ALL BAD
. . . CAN IT?

When it ends,
there are some
good things —

           Like more time
           to get work done,

           pay attention to
           the rest of the world,

           write about other
           subjects,

           reduce dependency,

           live in pain
             (whoops)

JUST A THOUGHT

the time has come
he said to her
to talk:

of life's realities
and time's passage,
of what has been
what is
what is to come,

of fear that makes
us shiver in the heat,
of joining and parting,
of re-joining or maybe not,
of fear that makes
us shiver in the heat.

love's an accident that
comes and must not be missed;
it incises a tattoo forever
upon the heart, leaves a
memory to float in and out
of consciousness at
unexpected moments,
for a longlong time.

LOVE'S OLD SWEET SONG

I.

They slammed into the wall,
both of them at the same time.

Bleeding internally, they tried
the climb, but

Fell away, once and again.

II.

In a dream or reverie
he ducked in a trench
lined with bones and fat worms.

Peering over the top, he saw
her, running toward him,
legs torn by barbed wire,
spurting red.

III.

He climbed out, ran toward
her, she moved — accelerating —
backwards, like a film in reverse.

He screamed out "Darling!" as she
disappeared under the horizon.

He put his pistol between his lips
and, as torrents of rain sheeted across
the battlefield, the world turned crimson.

VERNALLY YOURS

Spring is come again
and three times alive:
For you
for me
for us.

Sun's rays warming now enough, my love,
to thaw the wintry spirit of my soul,
and lead me down a narrow twisting path
to view the living entities of God.

To enter bubbling mountain streams
where even water-breathing creatures feel anew
the swell and surge of passion's beat.

And while we opt to feed upon their flesh,
we can't digest their simplest truth:
There is such difference
between what's base and basic
inside us.

But till we've learned to distill beauty from the beast,
let's keep our tryst beside that sun-warmed brook,
where life's a moving force that speeds our blood
assuring us tomorrow's joy is real.